D1566614

# The Architecture of
# Frank Lloyd Wright

**Understanding the Concepts of Parallel and Perpendicular**

Janey Levy

# PowerMath™

The Rosen Publishing Group's
## PowerKids Press™
New York

Published in 2005 by The Rosen Publishing Group, Inc.
29 East 21st Street, New York, NY 10010

Book Design: Michael J. Flynn

Photo Credits: Cover © SuperStock; pp. 5, 13 © Bettmann/Corbis; pp. 7, 19, 27 © Thomas A. Heinz/Corbis;
pp. 8 (inset), 30 © Angelo Hornak/Corbis; pp. 8–9 © Lee Snider/Corbis; p. 10 © Sandro Vannini/Corbis;
p. 11 © Corbis; pp. 14–15 © Richard Hamilton Smith/Corbis; pp. 17, 18, 29 © Farrell Grehan/Corbis;
p. 21 courtesy of Martin Family Photographs, Margaret Foster Collection 453, Box 4, Frank Lloyd Wright
Collection, University Archives, University at Buffalo, State University of New York; pp. 22, 23 courtesy
of Martin Family Photographs, Fuermann 58, Box 7, Frank Lloyd Wright Collection, University Archives,
University at Buffalo, State University of New York; pp. 24–25 © Richard A. Cooke/Corbis; p. 26 © Leonard
de Selva/Corbis.

Library of Congress Cataloging-in-Publication Data

Levy, Janey.
  The architecture of Frank Lloyd Wright : understanding the concepts of parallel and perpendicular / Janey
Levy.
       p. cm. — (PowerMath)
  Includes index.
  ISBN 1-4042-2940-X (library binding)
  ISBN 1-4042-5144-8 (pbk.)
  6-pack ISBN: 1-4042-5145-6
  1. Wright, Frank Lloyd, 1867-1959—Criticism and interpretation—Juvenile literature. 2. Architecture—
United States—20th century—Juvenile literature. I. Title. II. Series.
  NA737.W7L48 2005
  720'.92—dc22
                              2004003248

Manufactured in the United States of America

# Contents

Frank Lloyd Wright, American Architect     4

A New American Architecture     6

Euclid's Geometry     12

Prairie Style Houses     16

Fallingwater     25

Usonian Houses     28

The Spiral of the Guggenheim Museum     30

Glossary     31

Index     32

# Frank Lloyd Wright, American Architect

Frank Lloyd Wright was born in Richland Center, Wisconsin, in 1867, and began his work as an **architect** around 1886. His career spanned more than 70 years. During this time, Wright designed more than 1,000 structures—including houses, offices, hotels, churches, schools, libraries, and museums—although only about half of these were ever built.

Many people think that Wright was the greatest American architect of the twentieth century. He rejected the most popular architectural styles of the day, which were based on European architecture of earlier centuries, and devoted himself to creating a new, distinctly American architecture. Wright believed that an American architecture should express the nation's **democratic** values. This meant that houses should be of a modest scale that people could afford and would feel comfortable in. The new architecture should also be in harmony with the landscape. To Wright, this meant it should be in harmony with the order governing the universe, which he believed followed the rules of geometry. Wright tried to re-create this order in his buildings by emphasizing parallel and perpendicular (pur-puhn-DIH-kyuh-luhr) forms. Parallel forms extend in the same direction, are always the same distance apart, and never meet. Perpendicular forms meet at right angles.

This photograph, taken in 1957, shows Frank Lloyd Wright with a sketch for an office building he designed for the shore of Lake Michigan in Chicago. The building would have had 528 stories and would have been 1 mile tall!

5

# A New American Architecture

We can see how Wright used parallel and perpendicular forms to create a new American architecture by looking at the first house he designed after opening his own architectural firm in 1893. That year, Wright designed a house for William Winslow in River Forest, Illinois. Wright chose a basic geometric form for the Winslow House: a simple rectangular box. By definition, a rectangular box is composed of parallel and perpendicular planes. Opposite sides are parallel to each other. Sides that meet each other are perpendicular.

Wright favored **horizontal** structures, and the Winslow House is wider than it is tall. Wright further emphasized its horizontal quality by using different colors for the first and second stories. This makes it look as if the building is composed of 2 very long, narrow, rectangular boxes stacked one on top of the other. The low roof, which has gently sloping sides, projects well beyond the walls of the house. This emphasizes the house's horizontal quality. Parallel light bands along the lower edge of the roof and between the first and second stories also emphasize the horizontal quality. The perpendicular lines of the white window frames and the large white rectangle surrounding the entrance draw our eyes to these features. The result is a house that looks almost as if it were built out of building blocks.

Wright believed that a house should reflect the needs of its owners, the physical features of the place where it was built, and the natural materials—types of wood and stone—found in that location.

Winslow House
▼

◄Gothic church

spire

gable

pointed
arch

To get an idea of what made Wright's designs special, let's compare the Winslow House with 2 other buildings that were constructed around the same time. We'll compare it to a house built in the popular Gothic revival style and a building done in the popular **neoclassical** style.

Let's look first at the Lyndhurst mansion, which was built in 1880 in the Gothic revival style. A revival style is one that copies a style used in the past. Gothic revival imitates the original Gothic style, which was used for churches and palaces in Europe from about 1200 to about 1500. Like structures built in the Gothic style, the Lyndhurst mansion had windows with pointed arches; short, square towers; triangular **gables**; and many small **spires**. Gothic revival buildings also had irregular shapes. They seem to be made up of units of different heights, shapes, and sizes that were stuck together without any particular plan. The elaborately decorated Lyndhurst mansion is quite different from the simple rectangular shape of the Winslow House, shown on page 7.

The Lyndhurst mansion, located in the Hudson River valley, was the summer home of a wealthy businessman named Jay Gould. Compare its windows, towers, gables, and spires to those of the Gothic church shown in the small picture.

◀Lyndhurst mansion

Now let's look at a neoclassical building. Neoclassicism was modeled on Italian **Renaissance** architecture, which was in turn based on the architecture of ancient Rome and Greece. The style was popularized in the United States by the **Columbian Exposition** of 1893. Fair buildings like this one had Italian Renaissance features such as large arched windows, columns, sculpture on the roof, and huge, fancy domes. This rich decoration was meant to impress people and to make them feel wonder and admiration.

Also notice the size of this fair building compared to the people in the photograph. The building was enormous. It was meant to overwhelm people with its immense size rather than to create a setting in which people would feel comfortable. In contrast, the Winslow House shown on page 7 seems like a cozy, welcoming place where people could relax and feel safe.

St. Peter's ▶

Perhaps the most famous building of the Italian Renaissance was the church of St. Peter's in Rome. St. Peter's has arched doorways, many columns, sculpture on the roof, and a huge, fancy dome on top. Like the World's Fair building, it is also enormous.

◄ Columbian Exposition building

# Euclid's Geometry

The geometric elements Wright emphasized in his buildings are most closely associated with the ancient Greek mathematician Euclid (YOU-kluhd). Here are some definitions based on Euclid's famous book on geometry, titled *The Elements*.

A point has no length, width, or depth. •

(Don't confuse the dot we make to represent a point with the point itself. The dot is only a symbol for a point. Having a visible symbol makes it easier for us to work with the idea of "point.")

A line extends infinitely in both directions.
It has length, but no width or depth.

(Like the dot we make to represent a point, the line we draw is only a symbol for the idea of "line.")

It is possible to draw a straight line through any 2 points.

A surface (or plane) extends infinitely in all directions. It has length and width, but no depth.

Parallel lines are straight lines that lie in the same plane and never meet each other, no matter how far they are extended.

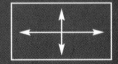

When one straight line meets another straight line in such a way that angles next to each other are equal to one another, each angle is a right angle, and the lines are perpendicular to each other.

All right angles are equal to each other.

Euclid was born around 325 B.C. and died around 265 B.C.

13

Of all the geometric forms discussed by Euclid, Wright most often emphasized parallel horizontal forms and the **vertical** forms that were perpendicular to them. This approach to architecture grew out of Wright's love for the landscape of his home state of Wisconsin and his belief that architectural forms should be in harmony with the landscape.

Wisconsin is part of North America's prairie region. It has low, rather flat land that sometimes seems to stretch forever. Occasionally, trees stick up at right angles—or perpendicular—to the prairie around them. Wright's buildings often repeated this geometry, creating a bond between the building and landscape that Wright felt was fundamental to the best architecture. Because of its association with the prairie, this early style of Wright's is known as the "Prairie style." Wright himself often referred to his architecture as "**organic** architecture" because it was based on the forms and order of the natural world.

This photograph of a Wisconsin cornfield gives a sense of the prairie landscape that Wright loved. Notice that the sides of the road are parallel to each other and that the silos near the distant barn are perpendicular to the horizon.

# Prairie Style Houses

Some people think the 1893 Winslow House was Wright's first house built in the Prairie style. Others believe the Ward Willits House, built around 1901 in Highland Park, Illinois, was the first true Prairie house. Like the Winslow House, the Willits House has 2 stories, with a roof that projects horizontally beyond the walls of the house. However, the Willits House is not a simple rectangular box. It is a more complex shape, consisting of a rectangular central space with a rectangular wing projecting from each side of that space.

By itself, this shape does not give the Willits House the same horizontal quality the Winslow House had. Wright created this quality in the Willits House by adding elements that run parallel to the ground and stretch out well beyond the wings of the house. On one side, a long, low roof projects from the entrance hall to form a covered parking area for a car. On the opposite side, a long, low roof covers a porch that extends from the dining room. On the front of the house, a walled terrace extends from the living room.

In the bottom image on page 17, parallel and perpendicular lines have been added to the photograph of the Willits House to clearly show how Wright used these geometric concepts in his work.

Wright's own words reveal the importance he placed on horizontal forms. In his autobiography, he described one of the houses he designed as stretching out horizontally "parallel to the ground." He went on to write that the house would be "a companion to the horizon."

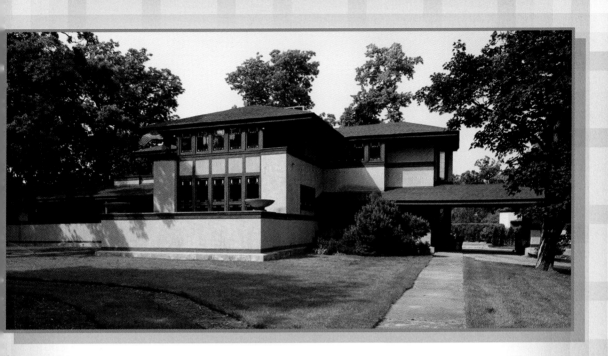

# Willits House

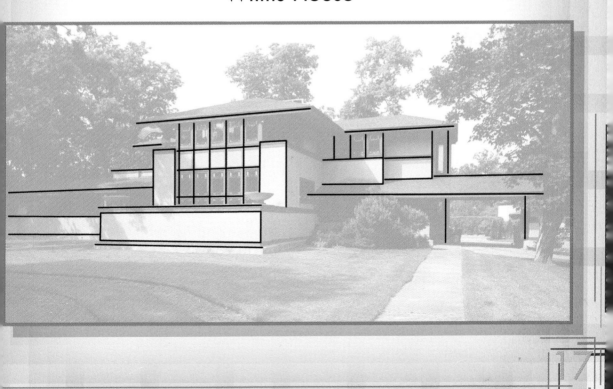

In the Willits House, Wright also gave greater importance to windows as a way to let sunlight and views of nature into the house. Five tall rectangular windows, side by side, turn the lower part of the living room wall facing the terrace into a wall of glass. A ribbon of smaller rectangular windows wraps around the upper part of the living room walls. Rows of rich brown stone outline the windows and emphasize the perpendiculars formed by the **intersecting** horizontal and vertical lines.

Wright continued the band of brown stone that runs below the upper windows all the way around the house to make the structure look more horizontal. Bands of brown stone along the top and bottom of the terrace wall repeat this upper band.

For the Willits House, Wright designed not only the house, but also the furniture in it and the art glass windows and light fixtures. In all of these elements, he repeated the parallel and perpendicular lines he used in the house itself.

The **art glass** shown below comes from a ceiling light in the dining room of the Willits House. It is decorated with a network of straight lines that run parallel to the sides of the square light fixture and intersect each other at right angles, creating a pattern of squares and rectangles of various sizes.

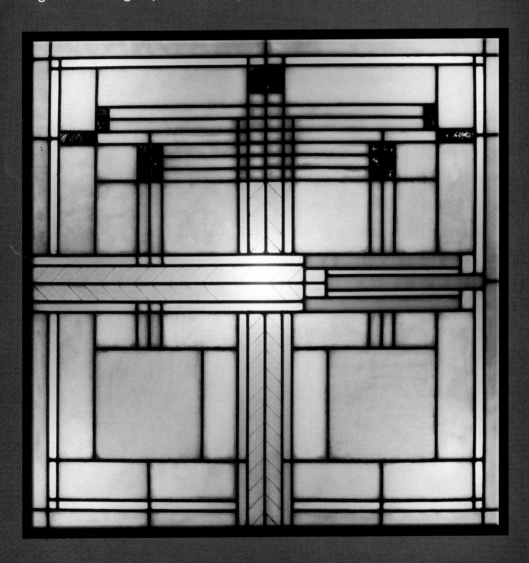

Another famous Prairie house is the Darwin Martin House in Buffalo, New York, built between 1904 and 1906. Some people consider it Wright's greatest Prairie house. Darwin Martin reportedly granted Wright an unlimited budget, which allowed Wright to design an unusually large home.

Wright made the Martin House larger by increasing its length rather than its height, creating a long, horizontal structure. Repeated parallel lines on the front of the house emphasize its horizontal quality. The horizontal line formed by the ridge of the low roof is repeated by the lower edge of the roof. Below that is a narrow band of windows, with a horizontal line of light-colored stone running along the windows' bottom edge. Below that is a horizontal roof that covers a long porch. A low brick wall topped by a row of light-colored stone hides the porch from view.

A section at the right end of the Darwin Martin House projects forward from the rest of the house. This section has thick pillars that are perpendicular to the house's horizontal forms, just as the tree in front is perpendicular to the ground.

Wright also designed 5 other buildings on the property occupied by the Darwin Martin House, including a house for Martin's sister and her husband and a cottage for Martin's gardener.

During construction, 50 men worked on the Darwin Martin House for 10 hours per day, 6 days a week. They earned $12 per week.

Darwin Martin House

As he did for the Willits House, Wright also designed furniture, art glass windows, and light fixtures for the Martin House. This photograph of a room in the house shows 2 art glass windows whose patterns of intersecting horizontal and vertical lines repeat the lines of the house itself. Unlike most people, Wright thought of windows as part of the wall rather than simply holes in it. He called windows "light screens" and made them part of the overall design of the house, not something conceived and designed separately.

The windows for the Martin House were made by the Linden Glass Company in Chicago, following Wright's designs.

There are also 2 chairs designed by Wright. In these chairs, all the angles are right angles and all the surfaces are flat planes. The legs and backs of the chairs are precise vertical lines that are all parallel to each other. Between the uprights on each side of the backs are several narrow strips of wood, all parallel to the uprights. The seats of the chairs are horizontal planes perpendicular to the legs and backs. Such chairs were probably not comfortable to sit in, but they were consistent with Wright's philosophy that all parts of a house should be in harmony with the geometric order of nature.

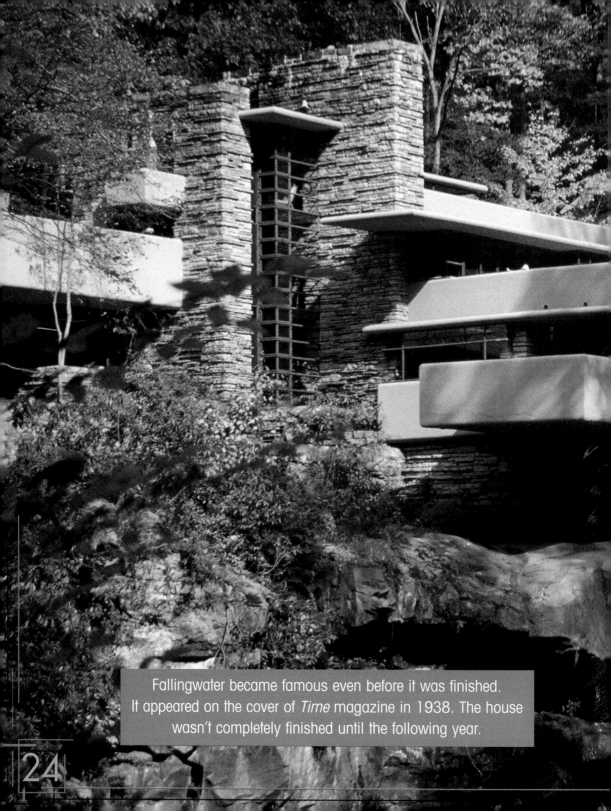

Fallingwater became famous even before it was finished.
It appeared on the cover of *Time* magazine in 1938. The house
wasn't completely finished until the following year.

# Fallingwater

In 1934, Wright began designing a house that has been called the most famous house in the world. The house, located in Mill Run, Pennsylvania, is called Fallingwater because it is built over a waterfall in Bear Run Creek. The people who hired Wright loved to picnic at the waterfall and asked Wright to design a house that would be perfectly suited to that spot.

The wooded hills and ravine make the site different from the wide-open prairie Wright loved. For the house to be in harmony with the landscape, something other than a Prairie house was needed. Wright created a daring design. Just as the rocks at the top of the waterfall stick out like a shelf over the ravine below, Wright designed the house to project from the hillside above the waterfall. This makes the house appear almost as if it's floating in space.

Fallingwater looks as if it is made of several flat slabs piled one on top of the other, much as the rocks of the hillside below it are layered on top of one another. The slabs vary in size and shape, just as the rocks do. However, Wright took the geometric order that he saw hidden in the irregular forms of the rocks and made the slabs of Fallingwater into regular rectangles.

The U.S. government honored Fallingwater by putting a picture of it on a postage stamp.

Frank Lloyd Wright 1867-1959 Fallingwater Mill Run PA

Architecture USA 20c

The sides of the rectangles vary in length, but the sides of each rectangular slab run parallel to those of the slabs above and below it, creating an ordered structure in the dwelling. Smooth, uninterrupted walls give each parallel layer of Fallingwater a strong horizontal quality. On one side of the house, stone chimneys rise perpendicular to the horizontal slabs, much as the trees rise from the surrounding landscape. Fallingwater exists in harmony with its natural setting.

# Usonian Houses

Wright believed that the harmony between architecture and nature that he had always sought in his designs could lead to a happier, more harmonious American society. He even had a special term for the ideal America he imagined—he called it "Usonia" (you-SOH-nee-uh), a name created from the first letters of "United States of North America." In the 1930s, Wright began to design homes he thought would help to create his ideal America. He called the houses "Usonian." They were small, modestly priced homes that the average person could afford.

To keep costs down, the Usonian houses needed simple designs that could be built quickly and easily. In the 1950s, Wright began to design **prefabricated** Usonian houses. The parallel and perpendicular lines Wright preferred were perfectly suited to prefabricated homes. The simple rectangular sections—or **modules**—of the houses could be easily constructed, shipped to the home site, and assembled. In the house shown here, parallel and perpendicular lines divide the windows and walls into numerous small rectangular units. These units are tiny versions of the modular sections from which the house was built and form the perfect decoration for the house.

A builder named Marshall Erdman constructed and sold the modular kits for Usonian homes. This home was built in 1957 for Walter Rudin of Madison, Wisconsin.

# The Spiral of the Guggenheim Museum

Throughout his career, Wright remained faithful to his belief that architecture should re-create the geometric order found in nature, though he did not always limit his geometry to parallel and perpendicular forms. He included curves and circles as well. In his daring final design, Wright used a **spiral** for the exhibit space of the Solomon R. Guggenheim (GOOG-uhn-hym) Museum in New York City. This complex geometric shape is also found in nature: Wright took his inspiration from a snail's shell.

The Guggenheim Museum was finished in 1959, the year Wright died. Had he lived longer, who knows what other exciting geometric shapes he might have used in his buildings?

# Glossary

**architect** (AR-kuh-tekt)  Someone who designs buildings.

**art glass** (ART GLAS)  Windows, light fixtures, and other glass objects designed to be decorative.

**Columbian Exposition** (kuh-LUHM-bee-uhn ek-spuh-ZIH-shun)  A name often used for the World's Fair held in Chicago in 1893.

**democratic** (deh-muh-KRA-tik)  Favoring social equality.

**gable** (GAY-buhl)  The triangular upper part of a wall under a sloping roof.

**horizontal** (hohr-uh-ZAHN-tuhl)  Parallel to the horizon.

**intersect** (in-tuhr-SEKT)  To meet and cross at a point.

**module** (MAH-jool)  One of a set of standardized units that make up a larger whole.

**neoclassical** (nee-oh-KLA-sih-kuhl)  Relating to a revival of the classical style of the Italian Renaissance or ancient Greece or Rome.

**organic** (or-GA-nik)  Of or relating to living things.

**prefabricate** (pree-FA-brih-kayt)  To make large sections of a building at a factory, so that construction only requires putting those sections together.

**Renaissance** (reh-nuh-SAHNS)  The name for the period in Italy from the 1300s to the late 1500s when there was a revival of ancient Greek and Roman art and architecture. The name comes from a French word that means "rebirth."

**spiral** (SPY-ruhl)  A curved shape that starts at a center point and curls out from it in wider and wider arcs.

**spire** (SPYR)  A tall, narrow pyramid atop a tower or pillar.

**vertical** (VUHR-tih-kuhl)  Straight up and down, perpendicular to the horizon.

# Index

**A**

America(n), 4, 6, 14, 28

**C**

Columbian Exposition, 10

**E**

*Elements, The,* 12
Euclid, 12, 14

**F**

Fallingwater, 25, 26, 27

**G**

geometry(ic), 4, 6, 12, 14, 16, 23,
      26, 30
Gothic revival, 9
Guggenheim Museum, 30

**H**

harmony, 4, 14, 23, 25, 27, 28
horizontal(ly), 6, 14, 16, 18, 20, 22,
      23, 27

**I**

Illinois, 6, 16
Italian Renaissance, 10

**L**

landscape, 4, 14, 25, 27
Lyndhurst mansion, 9

**M**

Martin, Darwin, 20
Martin House, 20, 22

**N**

nature(al), 14, 18, 23, 27, 28, 30
neoclassical, 9, 10
New York, 20

**O**

order(ed), 4, 14, 23, 26, 27, 30

**P**

Pennsylvania, 25
Prairie house, 16, 20, 25
Prairie style, 14, 16

**U**

Usonia(n), 28

**W**

Willits House, 16, 18, 19, 22
Winslow House, 6, 9, 10, 16
Winslow, William, 6
Wisconsin, 4, 14

AP 12 '07

J 720
LEVY
4/9/07
23.⁰⁰ LAR